ROMAN INVADERS

MILES
KELLY

PUBLISHING

First published in 2006 by
Miles Kelly Publishing Ltd
Bardfield Centre, Great Bardfield, Essex, CM7 4SL

Copyright © Miles Kelly Publishing Ltd 2006

2 4 6 8 10 9 7 5 3 1

Publishing Director:
Anne Marshall

Senior Editor:
Belinda Gallagher

Editorial
Assistant:
Ned Miles

Designer:
Louisa Leitao

Cartoons:
Mark Davis

Production:
Elizabeth Brunwin

ISBN 1–84236–656–4

Reprographics: Mike Coupe, Stephan Davis, Ian Paulyn,

Printed in China

British Library Cataloguing-in-Publication Data
A catalogue record for this book is available from the British Library

Indexer: Jane Parker

www.mileskelly.net
info@mileskelly.net

Contents

Celtic clans

enemies of Rome

The people who lived in Great Britain during Roman times were called Britons. Their language and way of life is known as 'Celtic'. The Celtic people lived right across Europe, from Spain to Turkey. Other Celts included the Gaels of Ireland and the Gauls of France.

Most Britons lived in small settlements of large, round houses made of clay, timber and stone.

The Britons belonged to many different tribes.  They were always fighting among themselves, and each tribe had its own king or queen and its own lands. There were important nobles, too, including priests and law-makers called druids. Most Britons were farmers and many others were blacksmiths and ironworkers.

Clothes were woven from linen and wool, and cloaks were fastened at the shoulder. Britons also liked wearing gold jewellery and the Romans thought they were show-offs,  forever boasting about how brave they were. Women wore long dresses and men wore tunics and trousers.

Celtic warriors fought with long spears and swords, and used horse-drawn chariots for speedy attacks.

Britons attacked

Roman rampage

In 55BC, a Roman fleet carrying 10,000 men approached the cliffs of Dover. Their commander, Julius Caesar, wanted to punish the Britons because they'd been supporting the Gauls, who had been fighting against him. Soon after the Romans came ashore, a storm blew up, damaging their ships. Caesar decided to sail home.

The first Roman to wade ashore was the standard bearer of the Tenth Legion. The other troops followed.

In AD42 the Roman emperor Claudius put together an army of over 40,000 men. Its aim was to bring the whole of Britain under Roman rule, once and for all. In the spring of AD43, Roman troops finally landed in Kent, led by General Aulus Plautius.

When ordered to invade Britain in AD43, the Roman troops went on strike, as they thought the Channel shore was the edge of the human world!

STONE THE HENGE! MEN IN SKIRTS!

YUK!

QUICK! LEG IT LADS!

CALLING ALL CELTS... RUN FOR YOUR LIVES!

PUFF

The Romans broke through the ranks of tribes and captured Colchester. Eleven tribes finally surrendered.

Celtic rebels
killer queen

In their first summer in Britain, the Romans made a big mistake.
They captured Caratacus, son of a Celtic king. However, he escaped and joined tribes in Wales where he led many attacks on the Romans. When Caratacus was finally defeated in AD51, he fled to the Brigantes tribe. The queen of the Brigantes handed him back to the Romans.

Caratacus escaped, but was handed back to the Romans. He was taken to Rome as a prisoner of war.

In AD60 the Romans attacked the druids (Celtic priests) of Mona. They were all slaughtered.

Boudicca, queen of the Iceni, attacked Colchester, London and St Albans. She was eventually defeated.

Rule Britannia

a new era

Britain became 'Britannia'. It was now a province of the mighty Roman empire, with its capital at Londinium, and was ruled by a governor. The province was divided into territories, military settlements and towns. Each had a council and elected magistrates to enforce the law.

The Roman army kept control. They set up military camps and strong forts built of timber and stone.

More Britons took up Roman customs. In the countryside, the old Celtic way of life carried on as before.

Many Romans moved to Britannia from Italy. They included doctors, servants and upper-class ladies.

Hitting the road
take a hike

The Romans introduced the first planned road system in Britain. Some were minor routes, but others were up to 12 metres wide, straight and well-drained. The chief purpose of these roads was to allow legions of soldiers to march quickly from one part of the country to another. No better roads were built until the 1800s.

The most important travellers were official messengers who rode on horseback. They travelled at spee•

 Roads were made with whatever stone was locally available. Layers of broken flint and stone were laid as foundations. The surface was generally gravel, but it was sometimes paved. Roads were built by the army, using troops or slaves as labour.

Slow traffic would move onto the broad verges to let faster traffic, such as messengers, go by. Some travellers used fast, lightweight carts pulled by mules, while others rode in slower, horse-drawn carriages. Heavy goods were carried in wooden wagons hauled by teams of oxen.

The roads were centred around Londinium (London). Most branched out to important army towns.

Hustle and bustle

city life

The Romans built grand towns, often on the sites of Celtic capitals. Smaller towns sprung up around crossroads and rivers, as well as by the sea. Roman officials, traders, lawyers and craftsmen moved in first, followed by Britons who could afford to take up the Roman way of life.

DUMPED!

FOUR DOWN, ANCIENT EMPIRE...

KEY TO THE DOOR?

C'MON, YOU OLD NAG!

The Roman period saw the first proper towns in Britain, with paved streets and grid-planned housing.

London (Londinium) was sited on the banks of the river Thames, ideally placed for trade with the empire. A long wooden bridge spanned the river, and the city had a huge fort, town hall and market place. At its peak, Londinium had a population of around 45,000 people.

When Boudicca rebelled, Roman troops had to march at very high speed. They covered 400 kilometres in 14 days!

COME ON LADIES, YOU KNOW IT MAKES SENSE!

LOOKS GREAT IN ANY VILLA...

SNAP!

Towns were supplied with water by aqueducts (water channels). Drains and sewers kept towns clean.

The Romans worshipped many gods and goddesses. Jupiter was king of the gods, Venus was goddess of love, Mercury was messenger of the gods, Diana was goddess of hunting, and Saturn was god of farming. Every Roman knew stories about the gods. In these stories, gods would act like people – quarrelling and falling in love.

Beautiful temples were built so that people could make offerings and give thanks to the gods.

Mithras was the Persian god of light and he was very popular among Roman troops. He was often depicted slaying a bull. Many temples were built to honour Mithras, including one in London.

In the countryside, the Britons still worshipped the Celtic gods and goddesses. In fact, many Romans happily adopted these gods, too. This was because they were often similar to their own gods. They even built shrines to many of them.

Foreign religions grew popular in Britannia over the years. Some emperors were even worshipped as gods.

Frontier of defence
Hadrian's Wall

Great Britain formed the northwestern frontier of the Roman empire. The Romans never conquered Ireland, so most of the frontier followed the coastline. In the north of Britain however, it crossed the land, and was defended by a wall – Hadrian's Wall. Its aim was to keep out tribes on the northern side and stop them from making alliances with tribes on the southern side.

There were forts along the wall to guard crossing points. Patrols brought in tribe members for questioning

Emperor Hadrian gave his name to the great northern wall, which was begun in AD122. For the soldiers serving there, life must have been boring. When troops weren't building or digging, they had marches, weapons-training or drill on parade. In their spare time they hunted, gambled or wrote letters home.

he wall was about 4 metres high by 3 metres wide. It was defended by ditches and ran for 117 kilometres.

Home from home
luxury villas

Villas were large Roman country houses. They were usually built at the centre of a large estate, with orchards and fields of wheat, flocks of sheep or herds of cattle. Labour was provided by slaves. Villa owners were usually wealthy Romans, such as government officials or retired army officers, but some Britons also owned land.

AN APPLE A DAY...

OOOPS!

THE PERFECT COUNTRY HOME!

I THINK THAT'S WHAT'S CALLED SAVING YOUR BACON!

The first villas were simple farmhouses, but as Rome prospered they became more and more luxurious.

The estates also offered hunting with dogs. Deer were a popular choice as venison was often a welcome addition to the menu. Boar (wild pig) were common in Britain, and could become very dangerous if cornered. A charging boar could send a hunter flying and its sharp tusks could gash a leg badly.

Villa floors were decorated with mosaics, which are pictures made up of hundreds (or thousands) of tiny tiles, set in cement, to make pictures and patterns. It was common to see images of gods in these mosaics, as well as animals or fruit. Craftsmen would travel the empire laying mosaics.

ouses and gardens were decorated with shrines to the gods. It was believed these protected the household.

Hard day's work
the daily grind

Britons were famous for their pottery before the arrival of the Romans. However, under Roman rule, pottery-making became a big industry. The design of kilns (where pottery was 'fired' and hardened) improved greatly, and before long, dishes, jugs and kitchenware were being produced on a large scale.

Potteries sprung up wherever there was good clay. There were many in Oxfordshire and southern England.

The Romans could teach the Celts little about ironworking or blacksmithing, as it was their speciality. Business boomed as there was always work to be done – armour, weapons, axes, pans and horseshoes all needed making!

Roman ships have been found preserved in the mud of the river Thames. London's first wharves have also been discovered.

Weaving was a big industry under Roman rule. Work was done by hand, as there were no spinning wheels.

Learning and medicine
Roman style

The children of wealthier Britons and Romans went to school at age six or seven. At school they would learn reading, writing, history, sport and arithmetic. Most children left school around the age of 11 and some continued education at home.

At school, lessons would usually be very boring, and tutors would often hit students for wrong answers!

Girls would be expected to learn weaving and how to run a household as training for married life.

Medicine was basic, but doctors still treated eye infections and carried out operations.

Time to relax
when in Rome...

Every town had a public bath. Even wealthier Britons enjoyed bathing, too. Men and women bathed separately. People went to get clean, relax, have a massage or just chat with their friends. Any fair-sized town also had an open-air theatre where plays and gladiator fights were held.

Bathers covered their bodies in oil, then scraped themselves clean. Gladiators were slaves or prisoners.

The Romans loved playing games and gambling. The clatter of rolling dice could be heard in bath houses, inns and barrack rooms around Britannia. Playing boards were usually made of pottery, with little gaming pieces of bone, glass, clay or ivory.

Chariot-racers had the same following of fans as football stars do today. Everyone followed their favourite team!

GOOD SHOT!

SMACK!

W H O O S H H H!

OOPS... THAT'S BLOWN IT!

CHECK-MATE!

A popular game was 'Three Stones', which was like noughts and crosses. Children liked playing ball games.

Togas and jewels

looking good!

The most common Roman dress was a simple tunic, worn by workers, slaves and children. A woollen cloak would sometimes be worn for warmth. Important men wore a white robe called a toga, and men of high rank wore a purple-trimmed toga.

Hairstyles went in and out of fashion. Men usually had short styles. Women curled and plaited their hair.

Women wore lipstick, eyeshadow and face powder. Rich ladies wore jewellery of gold and pearl.

People wore sandals. Soldiers wore sandals with studded soles for marching. Boots were worn in winter.

Eating and drinking
Roman cuisine

Roman kitchens had ovens for baking bread, hearths for boiling and spits for roasting. Oil and other foods were stored in large pottery jars. Hung up in the kitchen you might find a hare or a duck. Spread out on the tables would be herbs, spices and vegetables.

MORE BOAR?

TIME FOR TOAST?

AND A NICE FRUIT SALAD.

THIS IS THE LIFE... BEING WAITED ON HAND AND FOOT...

Breakfast was usually just bread or fruit. Lunch might be leftovers from the night before.

At a Roman banquet, guests would eat lying on couches around a low table. Servants would bring in seven or eight courses. There would be starters, salads, dumplings, omelettes and shellfish. Main dishes consisted of kidneys, liver, roast venison in plum sauce or young goat cooked in cream.

I'M STUFFED

CHOMP!

LET'S OPEN ANOTHER BOTTLE!

THINK HE'S HAD TOO MUCH VINO COLLAPSO!

OOF!

Romans and wealthy Britons would have their wine imported from Italy, Gaul and Germany.

Index